EXPLORING
TRINITY

ONE GOD ...
OR THREE?

DOUG BATCHELOR

Exploring the Trinity: One God ... or Three?
By Doug Batchelor

Published by Amazing Facts, Inc.
P.O. Box 1058
Roseville, CA 95678
916-434-3880
afbookstore.com

Cover and text design by Daniel Hudgens
Text layout by Greg Solie • Altamont Graphics

ISBN: 978-1-58019-603-1

CONTENTS

INTRODUCTION

S pace is amazing; its sheer vastness is incomprehensible to the human brain.

In 1996, astronomers pointed the famed Hubble Space Telescope into a part of the sky that seemed relatively empty to regular earth-bound telescopes. To the human eye, the little patch of sky, adjacent to the Big Dipper, seemed no bigger than a grain of rice held out at arm's length.

Scientists kept the Hubble pointed at that spot for ten consecutive days. What it captured on its ultra-sensitive lens astounded researchers. The image produced by the data was one of the most profound and humbling in human history—every dot was an entire *galaxy*, a fiery pinwheel of light, each containing hundreds of billions of stars. Beginning in 2004, using much improved equipment, they pointed the Hubble toward a seemingly empty spot in the constellation Orion over a period of nine years. There, in the "blackness" of space known as the Ultra Deep Field, they found another 10,000 galaxies. It was the farthest into space that humans have ever peered.

One of the galaxies they found—called "Sombrero" because it looks like, well, a sombrero—is more than 31,100,100 light years away. That means that traveling at the speed of light (186,000 miles per second), it would take 31,100,100 years to get there. Sombrero itself is 50,000 light years across, meaning that it would take 50,000 years to go from one end of the galaxy to the other at the speed of light!

How do we wrap our minds around sizes and distances like these? It's simply beyond our comprehension. Yet the Bible says God can do it: "He counts the number of the stars; He calls them all by name" (Psalm 147:4). How humbling!

But, if all this weren't mind-boggling enough, astronomers now tell us that the vast universe we can see is only *four percent* of what is actually out there. That's right—just four percent! We still understand so little about the cosmos.

Think about this for a moment: With all the amazing breakthroughs in technology and space exploration, especially over the past two centuries, the universe is still full of mysteries, of things humans cannot see and cannot fully understand. How much more so would that be true about God, the one who created that universe?

It's a logical principle that a creator is greater and more complicated than whatever it has created. Rembrandt, for instance, was more complicated than his painting *The Storm on the Sea of Galilee*. Michelangelo was more complicated than his sculpture *David*, even though it was his timeless masterpiece.

Well, how deep, how vast, how powerful, how mysterious must be the God who created the universe? And if we can't fully understand the nature of that universe, how can we expect to fully understand the nature of the God who made it?

THE MYSTERIES OF THE MAKER

The simple answer is that we can't, and we shouldn't expect to, which is why perplexity over God's nature is nothing new.

Since the Creation, people have sought to fully understand Him and to fully explain Him, no matter how difficult that task is.

In the book of Job, Zophar uttered the cry of every human heart when he declared, "Can you search out the deep things of God? Can you find out the limits of the Almighty? They are higher than heaven—what can you do? Deeper than Sheol—what can you know?" (Job 11:7, 8). And no wonder the Lord says, "As the heavens are higher than the earth, so are My ways higher than your ways, and My thoughts than your thoughts" (Isaiah 55:9). Paul says God's ways are "past finding out!" (Romans 11:33).

Thus, when we study God and His nature, even as revealed to us in the surest way we can know Him—that is, through the Word of God— we must realize there are still things about Him that we are not going to fully understand. We are finite beings with sin-infected minds. It would be arrogant to think otherwise.

Therefore, we need to approach the mystery of His nature with a large measure of reverence and humility. As did Moses when he came into God's presence, we must take off our shoes, "for the place where you stand is holy ground" (Exodus 3:5).

Yet God has given us the Bible, and in it He has revealed to us truth that He has not revealed any-where else. And it's to the Bible that we turn—as peering through a magnificent telescope of truth, we explore the greatest and deepest mystery there could ever be, the nature of the God who created all that is.

◯ ONE NAME?

One of the most important scenes in the Bible, one that impacted the history of the world, is found in Matthew chapter 28.

Jesus had been raised from the dead after His crucifixion, just as He told His followers would happen. Though at first they doubted the stories of His resurrection, when He finally appeared to them in person, their faith in Him as the Messiah was affirmed and they were ready to do His will, wherever it would take them.

At the end of Matthew's Gospel, when the risen Jesus is with His followers, He gives them what

is commonly known as the "great commission."
He said,

> Go therefore and make disciples of all the na-
> tions, baptizing them in the name of the Father
> and of the Son and of the Holy Spirit, teaching
> them to observe all things that I have com-
> manded you; and lo, I am with you always,
> even to the end of the age (28:19, 20).

The question is, do these verses teach us anything about the nature of God?

The disciples, leaders of the early church, were
to go to the whole world and baptize people in the
"name" of the Father, the Son, and the Holy Spirit. Converts were not to be baptized in the name of
the Father only. Nor in the name of the Son only.
Nor in the name of the Holy Spirit only. No, they
were to baptize in "the name," the singular name for
all three; the Greek word for "name" here, *onoma*,
appears in the singular. All three under a singular
name? This text shows, indeed, the close relationship between the Father, the Son, and the Holy Spirit.

AGE-OLD QUESTIONS

What is the nature of that close relationship?

Is God the Father the only "one God"—or
is the Son, Jesus, God too? If so, do Christians

worship more than one God? Is that not polytheism, as some suggest? Is God the Father superior to Jesus? Did Jesus come after the Father? Was there a time when the Father but not Jesus existed?

And what about the Holy Spirit? Is He God too? If so, do Christians worship three gods, as Muslims claim we do? And just what or who is the Holy Spirit? How are we to understand the Holy Spirit in relationship to the Father and the Son? Is the Holy Spirit divine, or merely an impersonal force emanating from God?

From the early days of the Christian church to this very day, the subject of the Trinity has caused contention in the church. And no wonder, the church is made up of fallen finite beings trying to grasp the nature of a perfect and eternal God.

As we've discussed, even if God wasn't a triune being, it would be difficult to understand the full nature of God, a being who spoke—*spoke?*—the world into existence. How do we even begin to grasp His power and personhood, trinity or no trinity? And if, as we believe, we're going to spend an eternity learning about God, we shouldn't be surprised if some things about Him remain hard for us to comprehend now.

Yet this is a deep and important subject that this short book seeks to explore. By laying aside our preconceived ideas, opinions, and training, we can go directly to God's Word and learn what He has revealed about Himself. Even though we may not be able to comprehend all aspects of this topic, we should try to understand the scriptural teaching regarding it.

After all, the Bible has spoken to us directly on the nature of the Father, the Son, and the Holy Spirit. It has also said, as we will see, a lot on this topic. I believe this means that God does, indeed, want us to understand, to the degree that finite beings can, what He has revealed to us in His Word. Otherwise, why put it in the Bible?

AN ANCIENT *AND* CONTEMPORARY ISSUE

It was a meeting of influential Christian leaders and theologians. They had come together to debate a serious topic: the relationship between Jesus and the Father. That is, they were discussing the Trinity. (We'll look at this specific term a little later.)

One church leader argued passionately, with what he believed to be incontrovertible evidence, that the Father was the supreme member of the Godhead and that Jesus was subservient to Him. After that speaker, another rose and spoke on the same topic. Yet he argued, contrary to the first one, and with what he believed to be indisputable evidence, that Jesus and the Father possessed equality—that Jesus was not subservient to the Father.

INTRODUCTION

Those who know church history might think this is a depiction of the famous council of Nicea in AD 325, when church leaders were debating the relationship between Jesus and the Father. But that's not the case. Instead, what you read was a …

"… brief synopsis of the proceedings of one study group of the Evangelical Theological Society, meeting in Washington, D.C., on November 16, 2006. Although the specifics of the debate were quite different from that which took place 1,681 years earlier, there are some interesting parallels. While the doctrine of the Trinity has been discussed throughout the history of the church, controversy on the subject has broken out anew-and among persons who hold the same basic view of the Bible's authority." [1]

Thousands of years after Jesus left the planet, Christians are still asking questions and disagreeing about this topic.

Even among members of the Seventh-day Adventist Church, the nature of the Trinity has become an issue of fierce debate. It is true that, in the church's earliest days, some Adventist writers took what is known as an "Arian" position regarding

---

1   Millard Erickson. *Who's Tampering with the Trinity? An Assessment of the Subordination Debate* [Kindle Locations 59-62]. Kindle Edition.

the Trinity. This view claims that Christ hasn't always existed; after He was brought forth, however, His divinity was given to Him by the Father. If this view were true, it would mean that Jesus is inferior to the Father—a view with which the Seventh-day Adventist Church has long disagreed.

Still, many Adventists are now trying to resurrect the views of those early pioneers, arguing that the doctrine of the Trinity comes from pagan Rome, an example of how Protestant churches have been infected by Roman Catholic heresy. Hence, all the more reason we need to accept, they argue, the position of those early Adventists who rejected the Trinity.

What should the church do?

THE DOCTRINE

Considering its outlier position among popular denominations, the Adventist Church today takes a rather mainstream position on the Trinity. In its official statements of beliefs, Belief Number 2, titled "The Trinity," states:

There is one God: Father, Son, and Holy Spirit, a unity of three coeternal Persons. God is immortal, all-powerful, all-knowing, above all, and ever present. He is infinite and beyond human comprehension, yet known through His self-revelation. God, who is love, is forever worthy of worship, adoration, and service by the whole creation. [2]

This agrees with most of the Christian world. In the work *Systematic Theology,* influential author and theologian Wayne Grudem writes, "God eternally exist as three persons, Father, Son, and Holy Spirit, and each person is fully God, and there is one God." [3]

God is one in essence yet three in person. How, though, can all three persons be "fully God" yet there be just one God? As I've stressed already, it's not going to be easy for us to fully grasp the nature of God. Nevertheless, there's a good reason that most Christians accept this teaching—because it is, indeed, found in the Bible. (And what rule declares that everything in the Bible, especially when it comes to the nature of God, must be easily understood?)

Some within the Adventist Church argue that just because other churches believe this doctrine, it's no reason that we should. After all, hasn't God raised up the Adventist Church to counter false teachings found in other churches, such as the immortality of

---

2   www.adventist.org/en/beliefs/god/trinity; the official *Seventh-day Adventists Believe* also states unequivocally that all three persons of the Godhead—the Father, the Son, and the Holy Spirit—are each fully and eternally God. See pages 23–77. Published by General Conference Ministerial Association, 2005.

3   Zondervan, 1994, p. 226

the soul or Sunday sacredness as the replacement for the seventh-day Sabbath? Hence, why should we believe in the Trinity just because others do?

But that's not why the church officially embraces the Trinity doctrine. Of course, just because others teach it doesn't make it correct. And yes, I believe that God raised up the Adventist Church to preach against error. But this doesn't mean that *everything* other churches teach is wrong. Many churches teach doctrines that we as Adventists fully accept, such as Christ's substitutionary death, His bodily resurrection, and salvation by faith alone.

My point in showing that other denominations believe in the Trinity isn't to prove that the belief is right, but to suggest that we are not alone in seeing it, and that other Christians also see a biblical foundation for the Trinity doctrine.

And the fact that the Roman Catholic Church also teaches the Trinity does not mean that it must be wrong. The Roman Church believes, for instance, that Jesus died on the cross to save humanity from its sins. Do we reject that doctrine just because Rome teaches it?

"TRINITY"

Another commonly heard argument is that the term "Trinity" does not appear in the Bible. That's right—it doesn't.

INTRODUCTION

One of the most crucial concepts in Scripture is the idea of Jesus taking upon Himself humanity, a truth powerfully expressed by the apostle Paul in Philippians:

> Let this mind be in you which was also in Christ Jesus, who, being in the form of God, did not consider it robbery to be equal with God, but made Himself of no reputation, taking the form of a bondservant, and coming in the likeness of men. And being found in appearance as a man, He humbled Himself and became obedient to the point of death, even the death of the cross (2:5–8).

One of the essential doctrines of Christianity is the idea of Jesus, from conception to death and even beyond, assuming our humanity. Jesus was fully human *and* fully God—another crucial doctrine that is hard for us to grasp. And yet this idea, called the "Incarnation," is never called the "Incarnation" in the Bible, yet the Incarnation is central to Christian theology.

We make the same claim for the Trinity. Though the term itself is not in the Bible, the concept is. And not just in the New Testament, where it is distinctly taught, but in the Old Testament as well. Hence, we believe in the doctrine of the Trinity not because others do, but because the Bible teaches it.

OLD
TESTAMENT

⬤ TO TEAR A PAGE OUT OF THE BIBLE

An evangelist once came to a town in order to hold an evangelistic series. Part of his advertisement had the following announcement:

> COME HEAR A SERMON ON THE ONE PAGE THAT NEEDS TO BE TORN OUT OF THE BIBLE!

As you could imagine, the ad caused quite the controversy—even if, in terms of promotion, it was genius. Many people came to the meeting the night that this particular sermon was to be preached.

The evangelist stood before the crowd, picked up the Bible, and held it up in front of everyone. They all sat transfixed, wondering what this preacher was going to do. Would he really tear a page out of the Word of God?

With the Bible in his outstretched hands, he said, "I am now going to rip out a page out of the Bible that does not belong there." The crowd collectively held its breath. He then opened a Bible before them, tore out a page, and held the ripped paper in the air.

"Yes," he said to the stunned audience, "this page, the page separating the Old Testament from the New, should have never been in my Bible!"

Whatever you might think of the theatrics, the evangelist had a point. The Christian church has a tendency to downplay the importance and relevance of the Old Testament. Many centuries ago, an important figure in the early church, Marcion of Sinope, rejected the God depicted in the Old Testament and would affirm only the God revealed in the New Testament. He argued that the God in the Old Testament was a mean, hateful, and vengeful deity in contrast to the loving, forgiving, and gracious God of the New Testament, especially as revealed in Jesus. Though Marcion's views were rejected early on, the idea behind it, that the Old Testament is inferior to the New Testament, finds tacit support among many Christians today.

Yes, the New Testament is, in many ways, a fuller revelation than the Old Testament. But the Old Testament forms the foundation of the New Testament. Of course, when we say that the New Testament is fuller, we mean its teachings are more fleshed-out expressions of the truths first revealed in the Old Testament.

Hence, to better understand the great truths found in the New Testament, we must see how they were first taught in the Old Testament. From Creation, to sin, to redemption—they're all there, revealed in the Old Testament by the Hebrew prophets. And among the great truths first revealed in the Old Testament is the doctrine of the Trinity. Let's discover how.

⬤ SHEMA YISRAEL

To this day, religious Jews often recite a line—called the *Shema*—from the Old Testament: "Shema, Yisrael, Adonai Elohanu, Adonai Echad."

Translated, it says: "Hear, O Israel: The LORD our God, the LORD is one!" (Deuteronomy 6:4). This is a rallying cry, a mantra of sorts—something similar to America's "One Nation Under God" pledge. Centuries ago, when Jews were threatened with death for not converting to Christianity, many would willingly go to the gallows while chanting the *Shema*.

This verse is also used as the key text for the concept of monotheism, the idea that there is only one God—as opposed to the pantheon of gods that pagan nations around ancient Israel worshiped. Numerous Old Testament texts are explicit about this idea: Only one God, Yahweh, the Lord of the Hebrews, is real; all other gods are false and non-existent.

"To you it was shown, that you might know that the LORD Himself is God; there is none other besides Him. … Therefore know this day, and consider it in your heart, that the

LORD Himself is God in heaven above and on the earth beneath; there is no other" (Deuteronomy 4:35, 39).

Here are a few more: "I am the LORD, … there is no God besides Me" (Isaiah 45:5). "I am God, and there is no other; I am God, and there is none like Me" (Isaiah 46:9).

Of course, the *Shema* has also been used to argue against the Trinity doctrine. God is one, so how could the Father, the Son, and the Holy Spirit all be God? Yet Christians who believe in the Trinity believe in one God only, even if that God is made up of three fully divine persons—a concept that the *Shema* does not specifically address. The point of the *Shema* was to help Jews differentiate their one God from the plurality of pagan "gods" worshiped by their neighbors.

In other words, the *Shema* wasn't addressing the nature of Yahweh as much as it was pointing out His distinctiveness from other deities. Indeed, the direct references in the Old Testament to the oneness of God are always presented as a contrast between God and false pagan deities, such as those of the Canaanites. The contrast is never about the idea of a one-being God versus a plurality within one God. The purpose was for excluding polytheism.

⚪ THE PLURALITY OF ONE

Moreover, some have found "hints" for the plurality of God within the *Shema* itself. One of the more interesting is that the word for "one" in Hebrew, *echad,* can be used in situations in which something called "one" is composed of various parts.

For instance, Exodus 24:3 reads, "Moses came and told the people all the words of the LORD and all the judgments. And all the people answered with *one* voice and said, 'All the words which the LORD has said we will do'" (emphasis added). Notice that it says that the people answered with "one," *echad*, voice. Yet how many hundreds of thousands responded? Here the idea of "one" represents unity—a composite of beings functioning as one.

Genesis 2:24 says that "a man shall leave his father and mother and be joined to his wife, and they shall become *one* flesh" (emphasis added). The Hebrew word for "one" here is, again, *echad,* referring to the idea of one, yes, but a one that is composed of two distinct parts—a husband and a wife functioning as a composite unity—a unit of one, *echad.*

Genesis 1:5, in the American Standard Version, reads: "God called the light Day, and the darkness he called Night. And there was evening and there was morning, *one* day" (emphasis added). This first day was composed of two parts, an evening and a morning, and yet it was one, *echad,* day.

My point here is to show that the idea of one, *echad,* as expressed in the *Shema* allows for a plurality within that oneness. What the text does not do is refute the Trinity. And in John 17:11, Jesus prays that the apostles can "be one as We are." The word "one" in Greek means "a single unit" and is often used numerically, but Jesus is praying the apostles will be one in purpose.

◯ LET US ...

The concept of the plurality of God is even seen in the Creation account:

> God said, "Let Us make man in Our image, according to Our likeness; let them have dominion over the fish of the sea, over the birds of the air, and over the cattle, over all the earth and over every creeping thing that creeps on the earth" (Genesis 1:26).

For starters, though it's the preference of the translators, notice how the text has the words "Us" and "Our" capitalized, as is typically done for references to deity. But who is the "Us" referred to here? Why does Scripture put in the mouth of a monotheistic God a plural reference in regard to Himself?

This plurality becomes even more fascinating when compared to the following texts that appear in Genesis 11, when the people were scattered after the Flood and talked about building a city. They said, "Come, *let us* make bricks and bake them" (Genesis 11:3, emphasis added).

Let *us* make bricks—as in plural, as in more than one, just as in Genesis 1:26 when the Lord was talking about Himself as a plurality. The same thing occurs in the next verse, Genesis 11:4: "Come, *let us* build ourselves a city, and a tower whose top is in the heavens; *let us* make a name for ourselves" (emphasis added). Again, "Let us." Here the phrases imply more than one, an entire nation of people. Yes, there were many, but the many were functioning as one.

Again, in the Creation story, we have the same kind of language—plurality—used by God in reference to Himself. "Let Us make man in Our image, according to Our likeness" (Genesis 1:26). Why would God use this language if not pointing to His plural nature? Otherwise, its use here makes little sense; indeed, what else could it mean?

The idea that this is God talking to angels, for instance, has long been refuted, even by Jews who obviously reject the Trinity. Angels are created beings. Nothing in Scripture gives the idea that angels can create out of nothing, especially humanity.

The biblical depiction of the creation of man and woman reveals it was an act by God alone.

God alone, the One God, is the Creator, a theme expressed in John chapter 1 when referring to Jesus: "All things were made through Him, and without Him nothing was made that was made" (v. 3). After specifically referring to Jesus as God, the writer says that anything that was made, that is, anything that once didn't exist but then came into existence, did so only through Jesus, who "was God" (John 1:1).

In short, though Genesis 1:26 does not *prove* the Trinity, it provides striking evidence for the plurality of the one, *echad,* God. Yet this isn't the only place in the Old Testament where this plural reference to one, *echad,* God is found.

For example, after the fall, "The LORD God said, 'Behold, the man has become like one of Us, to know good and evil'" (Genesis 3:22). The phrase "LORD God" is *Yahweh Elohim,* the most formal name and title of God. *Yahweh* is the name of God; *Elohim* is a plural noun meaning "God." A great deal has been written about the use of the plural form for the word "God," which we won't get into here. But note that the verb "said" in the phrase "The LORD God said" is singular. It is the one, *echad,* God, who is speaking.

And this one God says "man has become like one of *Us*." Again, why the use of the plural pronoun here in reference to Himself? We have one, *echad,* God, *Yahweh Elohim,* talking about Himself, and yet He is doing so in what is, undeniably, a plural sense.

The only reason is that although God is one, He is a plurality.

Consider this analogy: One water molecule is made up of two hydrogen atoms and one oxygen atom. These are three distinct parts. And yet it is still just one water molecule, despite the triune nature of that one water molecule. Couldn't the same be said of one God made of three distinct parts?

Let's now jump to Genesis 11, the story of what people were doing after the Flood. As we've already seen, in talking about themselves, these people used the phrases "Let *us* build" and "let *us* make a name." What does God say in response? "Indeed the people are one and they all have one language. ... Come, let Us go down and there confuse their language, that they may not understand one another's speech" (Genesis 11:6, 7).

First, the Lord says that "the people are one." Again, the word for "one" here is *echad,* showing the plural nature of a body that, despite its plurality, functions as one. And we have the Lord, the one, *echad,* saying, "Come, *let Us* go down and there confuse their language" (Genesis 11:7, emphasis added). Again, we see God referring to Himself as a plural.

The strength of this plurality is lost a bit in translation. The text in the Hebrew more literally reads, "*let us* go down and *let us confuse* their language." The Hebrew word for "let us go down"—yes, it's one word—and the Hebrew word for "let us confuse" (also one word) are both in the same *plural* verb form!

Why would the Lord, who depicts Himself as one God, refer to Himself in all these places as plural unless, indeed, His oneness included the concept of plurality?

In Isaiah, we find a similar use of a plural pronoun by God to describe Himself. In vision, Isaiah writes: "I heard the voice of the LORD, saying: 'Whom shall I send, And who will go for Us?'" (6:8). Who will go for *"Us"?* Who is the "Us"? Though angelic seraphim appear in the vision, nothing indicates that they are being referred to here. It was the Lord talking about Himself, and doing so here, as in the other texts, in an unambiguously plural context.

Though these verses (Genesis 1:26, 27; 3:22; Isaiah 6:8) don't *prove* the Trinity, they show that the Old Testament—which introduces the idea of monotheism—certainly leaves room for this one God to be a plurality.

Nothing in the idea of oneness negates the concept of a plurality within that oneness. As with a water molecule, God is one, but He is composed of a plurality, even if that plurality is, unlike a water molecule, composed of persons, not atoms.

THE ANGEL OF THE LORD

There's more—and we're still just in the Old Testament! The phrase "the angel of the Lord" appears fifty-eight times in the Old Testament. A parallel phrase, "the angel of God," appears eleven times. The Hebrew word for "angel" is *malak,* which means, simply, "messenger." Hence, these few dozen references to "the angel of God" or "the angel of the Lord" are referring to a being other than God.

If the messenger of the king is not the king himself, then the messenger of the Lord is, certainly, not the Lord Himself. Or is He?

In a few passages, the distinction between the messenger of the Lord and the Lord isn't so simple. Indeed, in some cases no distinction exists; that is, the messenger or "the Angel of the Lord" is, in fact, the Lord Himself.

Confused? Take this episode found in Genesis 16:7–10:

The Angel of the LORD found her by a spring of water in the wilderness, by the spring on the way to Shur. And He said, "Hagar, Sarai's maid, where have you come from, and where are you going?" She said, "I am fleeing from the presence of my mistress Sarai." The Angel of the LORD said to her, "Return to your mistress, and submit yourself under her hand." Then the Angel of the LORD said to her, "I will multiply your descendants exceedingly, so that they shall not be counted for multitude."

What happened was that the angel of the Lord ("Lord" here is translated from the name of God, Yahweh) says to her, "I will multiply your descendants exceedingly." The "Angel of the LORD" speaks to her in a way that only God would speak; that is, the angel gives her the promise of many descendants. The angel doesn't say, "The Lord told me to tell you, 'I will multiply your descendants.'"

No, the Angel gives her the promise, similar to when the Lord Himself spoke directly to Abram and said, "I will make you a great nation; I will bless you and make your name great" (Genesis 12:2). Who but the Lord alone could make that kind of promise?

After the "Angel of the LORD" finished speaking, we read, "She called the name of the LORD [Yahweh] who spoke to her, You–Are–the–God–Who–Sees; for she said, 'Have I also here seen Him who sees me?'" (Genesis 16:13). The text says that it was the Lord, Yahweh, who spoke to her, and then she names Him as God. In this one verse, the text itself refers to the "Angel of the LORD" as God, and Hagar does the same.

It's clear from these texts that this "Angel of Yahweh," a distinct Personage in His own right, is also Yahweh Himself. However difficult it might be for us to grasp, if we accept the doctrine of the Trinity, then what's going on here becomes more understandable.

In the story of the burning bush, Moses was tending to his father-in-law's flock when the "Angel of the LORD" (Hebrew reads, "Angel of Yahweh") makes an appearance:

> And the Angel of the LORD appeared to him in a flame of fire from the midst of a bush. So he looked, and behold, the bush was burning with fire, but the bush was not consumed. Then Moses said, "I will now turn aside and see this great sight, why the bush does not burn." So when the LORD saw that he turned aside to look, God called to him from the midst of the bush and said, "Moses, Moses!" And he said, "Here I am" (Exodus 3:2–4).

Here is the same text, but this time with the Hebrew words for deity included in italics, instead of the English translation:

> And the Angel of *Yahweh* appeared to him in a flame of fire from the midst of a bush. So he looked, and behold, the bush was burning with

fire, but the bush was not consumed. Then Moses said, "I will now turn aside and see this great sight, why the bush does not burn." So when *Yahweh* saw that he turned aside to look, *Elohim* called to him from the midst of the bush and said, "Moses, Moses!" And he said, "Here I am."

In verse four, the word *Elohim* is Hebrew for God, the same word for God in Genesis 1:1—"In the beginning, *Elohim* created the heavens and the earth." Thus, if we look at all these texts—the "Angel of Yahweh" (v.2), Yahweh (v.4), and Elohim (v.4)—we can see they are all referring to the same God who manifested Himself to Moses in the burning bush.

All this becomes even clearer when, in verse 6, the Being first identified as "the Angel of the LORD" says to Moses, "I am the God of your father—the God of Abraham, the God of Isaac, and the God of Jacob." And Moses hid his face, for he was afraid to look upon God."

Later, in verse 14, when Moses asks what name he should call the Lord, the Bible says, "God said to Moses, 'I AM WHO I AM.' And He said, 'Thus you shall say to the children of Israel, "I AM has sent me to you." ' "

In short, in the story of the burning bush, the "Angel of the LORD" is identified as Yahweh, Elohim, and "I AM WHO I AM"—all undeniable references to God.

And these are not the only Old Testament passages where something similar happens (see also Numbers 22:31–38; Judges 2:1–4; 6:22). In Judges 6:22, Gideon refers to "the Angel of the LORD" as God: "Now Gideon perceived that He was the Angel of the LORD. So Gideon said, 'Alas, O Lord GOD! For I have seen the Angel of the LORD face to face.'"

For thousands of years, Bible students have wrestled with the meanings of these texts in regard to the identification, by the Bible, of the "Angel of the LORD" with God—which is problematic for those who don't allow for a plurality of persons in the Godhead. Do these texts by themselves *prove* the doctrine of the Trinity? No. What they do show, however, is that in Old Testament monotheism, a plurality of persons is not contrary to Scripture.

THE PLURALITY OF GOD IN THE OLD TESTAMENT

From what we have seen so far, the Old Testament allows for a plurality in God. That is, even amid its unrelenting monotheism, more than one person is referred to as God. In biblical thought, therefore, God as One does not mean God as singular. The strict monotheism of the Hebrew prophets does not preclude a plurality of persons within God.

This teaching is important because it sets the groundwork, the foundation, for the more complete revelation of the Trinity found in the New Testament. That is, when the New Testament unambiguously points to the plural nature of the Godhead, it does not introduce a radical new teaching. On the contrary, the New Testament gives this Old Testament concept a much clearer exposition.

NEW
TESTAMENT

◯ LOVE ALONE?

As Christians, we believe, based on a great deal of evidence, that God is a God of love—the greatest example of that love being the cross, as expressed in this most famous Scripture: "God so loved the world that He gave His only begotten Son, that whoever believes in Him should not perish but have everlasting life" (John 3:16).

But the Bible teaches something more about God. It says, "God is love" (1 John 4:8). It doesn't say in this text that God loves, though He does; it doesn't say that God reveals love, though He does. It says that God *is* love. The first examples talk about what God *does*; 1 John 4:8 talks about what God Himself *is*, a very different thing. The sentence "John speaks French" says something very different than the sentence "John is French."

Yes, God loves, and we can understand that love to some degree because we, made in His image, can reflect that love. But to say that God *is* love is to say something that, frankly, eludes our intellectual grasp. It's good news, for sure—certainly better than saying "God is hate"—but what does it actually mean?

Though much ink has been spent trying to explain this idea, for our immediate purposes, exploring the Trinity, God as love becomes a crucial concept.

Scripture is clear, in numerous places, that God is the Creator. All that came into existence came from Him. But what about the time *before* He created the world? What about the time when all that existed was God alone, before He had created anything at all, either in heaven or in earth—even the angels? If God was love before He had created anyone or anything, whom did He love? If nothing was there, what existed for God to love?

For this reason, theologians have talked about the necessity, if not of the Trinity per say, but of the plurality of God, because without it, the idea of God being love, or even loving, makes little sense. Love can exist only in a relationship with the one loving the object of that love. Hence, the idea of God as love indicates the necessity of His plural nature.

And in the New Testament, the reality of His plural nature becomes quite apparent.

MY BELOVED SON

One of the most powerful scenes in the New Testament is the baptism of Jesus:

> When He had been baptized, Jesus came up immediately from the water; and behold, the heavens were opened to Him, and He saw the Spirit of God descending like a dove and

37

alighting upon Him. And suddenly a voice came from heaven, saying, "This is My beloved Son, in whom I am well pleased" (Matthew 3:16, 17).

How fascinating that at the beginning of Jesus' earthly ministry, Jesus, the Father, and the Holy Spirit all manifested. In John 10:30, Jesus claims equality with the Father: "I and My Father are one." And in Acts 5:3, 4, the Holy Spirit is identified with God Himself. (In this story, after Peter accused Ananias of lying to the Holy Spirit, he repeats the charge, saying to Ananias that he had "not lied to men but to God." More on this later.) And now, at the baptism of Jesus, all three persons appear in this one place and at one time.

Though the passage found in Matthew 3:16, 17, doesn't *prove* the Trinity, it's not alone; it's just one of many others that, together, show the triune nature of the biblical God.

While this scene unfolded at the beginning of Jesus' ministry, we saw earlier that, at the end of His ministry, during the great commission, the Father, the Son, and the Holy Spirit appear, this time under one name: "Go therefore and make disciples of all the nations, baptizing them in the name of the Father and of the Son and of the Holy Spirit" (Matthew 28:19).

All three were bundled together under the "name," which is singular. Whose name? The name of God. But why would the Son and the Holy Spirit, if somehow unequal to the Father, be placed on the same level with the Father in this way? It would be blasphemous (which is what Muslims think) to have equated Jesus with the Father were the Savior a lower or inferior being. And the same holds true with the Holy Spirit. If He were just an impersonal force emanating from God, why put Him on the same level as the Father under the same one "name," a name in which people are baptized?

Thus, between the mutual appearance of the Father, the Son, and the Holy Spirit at the beginning of Jesus' ministry, and their being named together at the end of Jesus' ministry, we have been provided more evidence for the idea of the triune Godhead.

GOD, JESUS, SPIRIT

Even in the New Testament, where most of the biblical evidence for the Trinity is found, no single text fully explains it. (What crucial doctrine is ever fully illuminated by a single text?) However, using the Protestant principle of letting the Scripture interpret Scripture, using Bible texts to explain other Bible texts, a student of the Bible will find abundant evidence in the New Testament for the Trinity.

For example, reminiscent of the great commission's call to baptize in the name of the Father, the Son, and the Holy Spirit, the New Testament features numerous passages where these three persons are linked in a way that implies equality.

Since the Father sent the Son into the world (John 3:16), He cannot be the same person as the Son. Likewise, after the Son returned to the Father (John 16:10), the Father and the Son sent the Holy Spirit into the world (John 14:26; Acts 2:33). Therefore, the Holy Spirit must be distinct from the Father and the Son.

For example, Paul wrote "that I might be a minister of Jesus Christ to the Gentiles, ministering the gospel of God, that the offering of the Gentiles might be acceptable, sanctified by the Holy Spirit" (Romans 15:16). Jesus, God, and the Holy Spirit are here expressed together. In this text, the Spirit is the one said to sanctify. But isn't sanctification God's job? "May the God of peace Himself sanctify you completely" (1 Thessalonians 5:23). But there is no problem here if the Spirit is, indeed, equal to God.

Paul also wrote, "I beg you, brethren, through the Lord Jesus Christ, and through the love of the Spirit, that you strive together with me in prayers to God for me" (Romans 15:30). Here God, Jesus, and the Spirit are linked again. Let's look at that same text but switch the various places where the three persons are placed. That is, suppose it read like this: "I beg you, brethren, through the Spirit, and through the love of God, that you strive together with me in prayers to the Lord Jesus Christ for me." It would read just fine, would it not? And that's because all three persons are fully divine.

Here's one from Romans 14:17, 18: "The kingdom of God is not eating and drinking, but righteousness and peace and joy in the Holy Spirit. For he who serves Christ in these things is acceptable to God and approved by men."

Now look at 2 Corinthians 1:21, 22: "He who establishes us with you in Christ and has anointed us is God, who also has sealed us and given us the Spirit in our hearts as a guarantee." Once again, Christ, God, and Spirit are linked.

Second Corinthians 13:14 says, "The grace of the Lord Jesus Christ, and the love of God, and the communion of the Holy Spirit be with you all." Again, all three Persons together, which wouldn't make sense if the Son and the Spirit were inferior to God.

Philippians 3:3 says, "We are the circumcision, who worship God in the Spirit, rejoice in Christ Jesus, and have no confidence in the flesh." And 1 Peter 1:2 says, "Elect according to the foreknowledge of God the Father, in sanctification of the Spirit, for obedience and sprinkling of the blood of Jesus Christ." Here we see the close tie between God, Jesus, and Spirit, a closeness that doesn't make sense were the Spirit and Jesus inferior to the Father. Would it not denigrate the Father were He so closely tied to persons, or just a force, without that distinction being made? Instead, all three appear together—powerful evidence of their unity and equality.

Even the opening of Revelation contains references to the three persons of the Godhead:

> Grace to you and peace from Him who is and who was and who is to come, [God the Father] and from the seven Spirits who are before His throne [God the Holy Spirit], and from Jesus Christ, [God the Son] the faithful witness, the firstborn from the dead, and the ruler over the kings of the earth (1:4, 5).

THE CHALLENGES

In discussions about the nature of the Godhead, specifically the Trinity, the deity of the Father is, of course, never questioned. Those who reject the plural nature of God typically point to the Father as the one God, the God of Israel. He is the Lord, Yahweh. "Remember the former things of old, for I am God, and there is no other" (Isaiah 46:9).

It's the other two, Jesus and the Holy Spirit, whose deity and eternity is questioned, challenged, and denied. What are those challenges, and why has the Christian church largely rejected them? Why does the church insist that both Jesus and the Holy Spirit are as much God as the Father is God? Let's find out.

THE NON-EXISTENT JESUS?

One of the central challenges to the Trinity doctrine concerns Jesus. Was He fully God, one with the Father, from eternity? That is, did He, like the Father, always exist? This is the basic Trinitarian view of Jesus: He was fully divine, which means that He existed from eternity past just as the Father has.

Or, in contrast, was there a time when Jesus did not exist, as many have argued? If so, then Jesus, no matter how exalted, would still be a created being. This would mean that however different Jesus is in stature, importance, and authority from rabbits, rocks, and radishes, He shares one thing in common with them: He, too, is a created entity, someone who once didn't exist but then came into existence, just as rabbits, rocks, and radishes once didn't exist as well.

This difference would create a vast divide between Him and the Father. The Father is one who has always existed, one who, by nature, was vastly different than Jesus if, indeed, Jesus were created. It would be like the difference between Rembrandt and one of his paintings—even the one worth the most, the one deemed his greatest and most important. However fantastic that creation, it is in no way equal with Rembrandt himself. It is not even close.

It's the same with the Father and Christ. If Jesus were created, then however important Christ's role, whatever He did for humanity, He would still, of necessity, be something radically different than the Father. In His essence, as a created being, He would be more like rabbits, rocks, and radishes than God. Such a position would, it would seem, have powerful implications for the whole meaning of the gospel and the plan of salvation.

What, then, is the truth? What does the Bible teach about the nature of Jesus? Was He eternally God, or was He—no matter how exalted—still a created being?

IN THE BEGINNING

The common Greek word for "God" in the New Testament is *theos*, and it is often applied directly to God the Father. Yet this same word, *theos*, is used more than half-a-dozen times by Paul, John, and Peter to refer to Jesus. What do they teach us about Jesus' divinity?

One of the clearest texts on this is found at the start of John's Gospel. Talking about Jesus, he wrote:

> In the beginning was the Word, and the Word was with God, and the Word was God. He was in the beginning with God. All things were made through Him, and without Him nothing was made that was made (1:1–3).

All the Greek terms for "God" here come from *theos.*

Moreover, the phrase "in the beginning" points right back to Genesis 1:1: "In the beginning God created the heavens and the earth." God, *Elohim,* is the Creator, who, not dependent upon pre-existing matter, created the earth and all things in it. John, however, seems to take it further than just the earth, stressing that Jesus *is* the Word and that through Him all things were made "and without Him nothing was made that was made." That is, anything that once didn't exist—planets, stars, galaxies, angels—but then came into existence did so through Christ. Jesus is depicted as the Creator, one with *Elohim* in the act of the Creation.

For what John wrote to be true, Jesus could not have been made because He Himself created all "that was made." How could that include

Himself? You can't create yourself because you would have to already exist in order to do it. The logic alone of these texts makes the idea of Jesus as a created being impossible.

The text also says that Jesus, the Word, "was God." The Jehovah's Witnesses, who reject the eternity and divinity of Christ, translate this text as "the Word became a god." Despite deep grammatical problems with that translation, if true, Christianity would cease to be monotheistic, because Jesus became another kind of god, a created god as opposed to an eternal God. Suddenly, there would be two kinds of gods, and the essence of Trinitarian theology is that God is one God but composed of three equal persons—each fully and completely God.

Most important, and perhaps the main reason for these verses, is the powerful link here between His divinity and the Word; Jesus "was God" and He's human. Several verses later, after talking about Jesus as the Creator, John wrote: "The Word became flesh and dwelt among us" (1:14). Here we see the greatest mystery—that Jesus, the eternal God who created everything "that was made," took upon Himself our humanity.

In the context of the plan of redemption and its relationship to the broken law of God, Ellen White wrote in *Patriarchs and Prophets*, page 63:

In all the universe there was but one who could, in behalf of man, satisfy its claims. Since the divine law is as sacred as God Himself, only one equal with God could make atonement for its transgression. None but Christ could redeem fallen man from the curse of the law and bring him again into harmony with Heaven."

She also wrote, "In Christ is life, original, unborrowed, underived. 'He that hath the Son hath life' (1 John 5:12). The divinity of Christ is the believer's assurance of eternal life."[4]

If God created the law, and if the law *is as sacred as God Himself,* who alone but one equal to God could make atonement for it? If Rembrandt had committed a crime that demanded his death, would the destruction of one of his paintings, even his greatest and most cherished painting, instead of the death of Rembrandt himself, have satisfied the claims of the law?

Of course not. Hence, if Christ were anything but fully God, equal with God, He could not have satisfied the claims of a law as "sacred as God Himself." Even though she was looking at the eternal divinity of Christ from a different angle than was John, her words are a powerful confirmation of what John wrote about the eternal divinity of Jesus.

4   *The Desire of Ages*, p. 530

THE DAY OF JESUS

When the angels announced the birth of Jesus, they told the shepherds: "There is born to you this day in the city of David a Savior, who is Christ the Lord" (Luke 2:11).

The Greek word for "Lord" here is *kryios.* Interestingly, in Luke 1:76, when Zechariah the priest foretold the role of his son, John the Baptist, he quoted the prophet Isaiah, expressing it like this: "You, child, will be called the prophet of the Highest; for you will go before the face of the Lord to prepare His ways" (Luke 1:76). The word for "Lord" in the original Hebrew in Isaiah is Yahweh, the name of God, whom Zechariah calls "Lord," or *kryios,* is clearly talking about Jesus. Zechariah, under the inspiration of the Holy Spirit, referred to Jesus as *kryios*, "Lord"—the same word often used in the Septuagint, an ancient Greek translation of the Old Testament, to refer to Yahweh, God Himself.

Moreover, Jesus has been referred to as Lord other times in the New Testament. Acts, for instance, calls Jesus "Lord of all" (10:36). "All of" *what?* Maybe this Old Testament passage will help: "These are four spirits of heaven, who go out from their station before *the Lord of all the earth* (Zechariah 6:5, emphasis added)—that is, the Lord of all the earth. Now consider this one:

"It shall come to pass, as soon as the soles of the feet of the priests who bear the ark of the LORD, *the Lord of all the earth*, shall rest in the waters of the Jordan" (Joshua 3:13, emphasis added). To call Jesus "the Lord of all" or "King of Kings" makes sense only if He is fully God, because who else but God is "Lord of all"?

Talking about the day of judgment for someone doing evil, the apostle Paul wrote to "deliver such a one to Satan for the destruction of the flesh, that his spirit may be saved in the day of the Lord Jesus" (1 Corinthians 5:5). Paul is referring to end-time judgment, which He calls "the day of the Lord Jesus." (See also 1 Corinthians 1:8.)

The phrase "the day of the Lord Jesus" is, clearly, an echo of the Old Testament phrase "the day of the Lord," which appears many times in the prophets and is often depicted as a time of judgment. (In most cases, the phrase "the day of the Lord" is "the day of *Yahweh*.") Isaiah writes: "The day of the LORD [Yahweh] of hosts shall come upon everything proud and lofty" (Isaiah 2:12). Ezekiel writes: "The day is near, even the day of the LORD [Yahweh] is near" (Ezekiel 30:3). Joel writes: "The day of the LORD [Yahweh] is great and very terrible; who can endure it?" (Joel 2:11).

The point? Paul's phrase "the day of Jesus Christ" finds numerous parallels in the Old Testament phrase "the day of Yahweh," which makes sense only if Jesus was deemed by Paul to be equal with Yahweh. Otherwise, what Paul wrote would be blasphemous.

THE NAME OF JESUS

Also, in the time of Jesus, religious Jews gave powerful reverence to the name of God, Yahweh. The name was never spoken aloud, except by the high priest, and then only in the Most Holy Place on the Day of Atonement. Whenever the name, the four letters of Yahweh, YHVH, appears in a text, religious Jews pronounce the name *Adonai* (Lord) in its place. Even to this day, orthodox Jews refer to God as *Ha-Shem,* which means "the name." Indeed, some don't even like to spell out the word "God," replacing it with "G-d" instead.

This point becomes important because of the times the New Testament writers refer to the "name" of Jesus in ways that make sense only if He was God.

In Acts 2:21, for instance, Peter quotes the Old Testament prophet Joel: "It shall come to pass that whoever calls on the name of the LORD shall be saved." The Hebrew word for "Lord" is Yahweh. Peter quotes a Bible text that stresses that all who call upon "the name of Yahweh" will be saved, but then later, talking about Jesus, he declares: "Nor is there salvation in any other, for there is no other name under heaven given among men by which we must be saved" (Acts 4:12). Peter here equated the name of Yahweh with the name of Jesus in the context of who gives salvation and where salvation is to be found—a correlation that would be blasphemy *if* it were not true.

In fact, after quoting the book of Joel about calling upon the name of Yahweh, Peter in the same discourse wrote, "Repent, and let every one of you be baptized in the name of Jesus Christ for the remission of sins" (Acts 2:38). Salvation comes only from Yahweh, so Jesus here is being equated with Him.

New believers were baptized when the apostles preached "the things concerning the kingdom of God and the name of Jesus Christ" (Act 8:12). The name of Jesus Christ is, certainly, another name for the Lord.

I AM WHO I AM

When the Lord appeared to Moses in the burning bush, He identified Himself as "I AM WHO I AM" (Exodus 3:14). Though the exact meaning and pronunciation of the name YHVH is unknown, it's close in form to the Hebrew word translated in Exodus 3:14 as "I AM." (The capital letters come from the translators; biblical Hebrew has no capital letters.) The point is that we have here a direct reference to God and the only time where He calls Himself "I AM."

Bible students see places in which Jesus uses the phrase "I am" in ways that recall God's name. Without getting too deep into Greek grammar, we can say that, time and again, Jesus' "I am" quotes are expressed in a way that puts particular emphasis on the "I." A more literal translation might be: "I, I am." Even more powerful is that He used this expression in contexts that point to His divine nature as the great "I AM" of the Old Testament, Yahweh.

Take John chapter 8, for instance, during the Feast of Tabernacles, when the earthly temple was lit up to show how Yahweh had led the children of Israel for forty years through the wilderness. During this time, He had manifested Himself as a pillar of cloud by day and a pillar of fire by night. In this context, Jesus declared, "I am the light of the world. He who follows Me shall not walk in darkness, but have the light of life" (v. 12).

No question, the most dramatic of Jesus' "I am" quotes occurs when He had been in a discussion with religious leaders. He says, "Your father Abraham rejoiced to see My day, and he saw it and was glad." The leaders answered, "You are not yet fifty years old, and have You seen Abraham?" (vv. 56; 57).

How did Jesus respond? "Most assuredly, I say to you, before Abraham was, I AM" (v. 58).

In English, the phrase "I am" seems innocuous, but the reaction of the religious leaders tells us it meant so much more. "They took up stones to throw at Him" (v. 59). Why would they have tried to kill Jesus if they didn't believe what He said was blasphemous? He didn't say, "I am this" or "I am that." He said only, "I AM." They got the message: "The priests and rabbis cried out against Jesus as a blasphemer. His claim to be one with God had before stirred them to take His life."[5]

Writes theologian Paul Peterson, "Several of the other claims Jesus made when He used the phrase 'I am' imply a high degree of authority that normally belongs only to God. Jesus is 'the way, the truth, and the life. No one comes to the Father except through' Him (John 14:6). He is 'the resurrection and the life' (John 11:25) and 'the bread of life' (John 6:48)."[6]

Meanwhile, in Revelation 1:8, we read, " 'I am the Alpha and the Omega, the Beginning and the End,' says the Lord, 'who is and who was and who is to come, the Almighty.' " This is God Himself speaking. Yet in the same chapter, Jesus says about Himself: "I am the First and the Last" (Revelation 1:17), a direct quote from Isaiah 44:6: "Thus says the LORD, the King of Israel, and his

---

5   Ellen White, *Desire of Ages,* p. 470

6   *God in Three Persons—in the New Testament;* Andrews University, May 2015

Redeemer, the Lord [Yahweh] of hosts: 'I am the First and I am the Last; besides Me there is no God.'" Hence, Jesus is talking about Himself with language that Yahweh uses to talk about Himself. And as if all this weren't enough evidence, in Revelation 22:13, Jesus says, "I am the Alpha and the Omega, the Beginning and the End, the First and the Last."

None of Jesus' "I am" references or what He says in Revelation makes sense apart from Jesus being God; all the references, however, make great sense if He is. Ellen White wrote,

> The Captain of our salvation was perfected through suffering. His soul was made an offering for sin. It was necessary for the awful darkness to gather about His soul because of the withdrawal of the Father's love and favor; for He was standing in the sinner's place, and this darkness every sinner must experience. The righteous One must suffer the condemnation and wrath of God, not in vindictiveness; for the heart of God yearned with greatest sorrow when His Son, the guiltless, was suffering the penalty of sin. This sundering of the divine powers will never again occur throughout the eternal ages. [7]

----

7   Manuscript 93, 1899, 7BC, p. 924.

The "sundering of the divine powers"? What could that possibly mean apart from the eternal deity of Christ?

A FEW MORE REFERENCES

Meanwhile, what does one do with Philippians 2:5–7 apart from understanding it as a direct claim to the divinity of Jesus?

> Let this mind be in you which was also in Christ Jesus, who, being in the form of God, did not consider it robbery to be equal with God, but made Himself of no reputation, taking the form of a bondservant, and coming in the likeness of men.

The word "form" (*morphe*) means the essential nature of something, not just a facsimile or a copy. This truth becomes even more apparent with what follows: It was not wrong, it was not "robbery," for Jesus to be equal with God? How could that be true unless Jesus is, indeed, equal with God? The mathematical equation $2+2=4$ is another way to say that $2+2$ is equal with 4. If Jesus is equal with God, as $2+2$ is equal with 4, then He must be God and, certainly, not a lesser god—a god that came forth from the Father in the sense of having been created by Him. Were that true, He would not be equal to God. How could something created be equal to what created it? It just doesn't make sense.

Paul's point here was to show, among other things, what an amazing condescension it was on Christ's part to be equal with God yet take upon Himself our humanity. If Christ were a created being who later came forth from the Father, He could not possibly be equal with the eternal God. Ultimately, if He were not God, His condescension was from finite created being to another finite created being. Is that really so amazing?

And then there's Colossians 2:9: "In Him dwells all the fullness of the Godhead bodily." It doesn't get more divine than that, does it? How else does one make sense of this text apart from the full and eternal deity of Christ? In a created being, an inferior being, "the fullness of the Godhead" would not dwell. It's hard to imagine how much clearer Scripture could be on the eternal deity of Christ.

CHALLENGES

OBJECTIONS

As with any doctrine found in the Bible, such as hellfire, people can always find texts that could be construed to teach something else. It's no different with the eternal deity of Christ. Let's look at some of those in this section.

First, let me clarify that the understanding of Jesus as God does not mean that He is identical with the Father *as a person*. They are not the same persons, but two distinct persons, yet each one is fully God. When the Bible speaks about God, it doesn't automatically mean the Father, but the Godhead; the term "God" could refer to any of the persons of the Godhead. As with anything else in the Bible, context is key to knowing which person of the Trinity the Bible is speaking about.

One of the challenges in regard to the deity of Christ deals with the fact that Jesus became a finite human being; when in human flesh, He took on a subordinate role. That is, as a human being like us, while still our perfect example, He lived a life of submission to the Father, just as we are to do. He was fully God *but* also fully human—and it was in His humanity that He lived in submission to the Father as we are to live as well.

This concept helps explain texts such as:

"He went a little farther and fell on His face, and prayed, saying, 'O My Father, if it is possible, let this cup pass from Me; nevertheless, not as I will, but as You will'" (Matthew 26:39).

"I have come down from heaven, not to do My own will, but the will of Him who sent Me" (John 6:38).

"Though He was a Son, yet He learned obedience by the things which He suffered" (Hebrews 5:8).

"Do you think that I cannot now pray to My Father, and He will provide Me with more than twelve legions of angels?" (Matthew 26:53).

In His role as a human, coming to earth to be our example and our substitute, Jesus lived in complete submission to the Father. He had to—otherwise, what possible example could He be for us? What makes this all so astonishing is that He did while still fully divine. That's the precise message of Philippians 2:5–7.

THE SON

Some people, understandably so, have difficulty with the concept of an eternal Jesus being a "son," since the term implies someone who came after his parents.

But we need to tread carefully, understanding the limitations of human language in the midst of the divine. As we saw earlier, it's already difficult when using language to describe the expanse of the known universe. Imagine what those limits are when using human language to describe heavenly things!

For example, we say that God is our Father, but He is not exactly like a biological father, is He? After all, our father needed a mother, a woman, in order to make us. Our fathers had fathers who made them, but one certainly can't say that about God the Father. Thus, we have to watch how far we push human imagery and language when talking about God.

This becomes vital to the understanding of Jesus as "the Son." In biblical language, a son isn't always the direct male child of a father and mother. The term can also refer to descendants a few generations removed. It can also refer to students, as in "sons of the prophets" (2 Kings 2:3), who were not literally the sons of prophets. Indeed, "son" can refer to a successor in an office. Daniel called Belshazzar the son of Nebuchadnezzar, even though he wasn't the genetic child of Nebuchadnezzar (Daniel 5:22). A "son" in the Bible can often be a representative, as seen by the term "sons of God" in Job 1:6 and 2:1.

Jesus is called "the Son of God" … because of His role of representing the Godhead. In that sense Jesus was the eternal Son. He has always represented God to the created beings. He did that from eternity. Then, in the incarnation He became the "Son" in a special sense by taking upon Himself human nature in order to save what was lost. [8]

In other words, Jesus is the "Son of God," yes, but not a "son" in the way male children are sons to their fathers and mothers; that is, once not existing and, then, coming into existence. To push the meaning of the term "son" onto Jesus that far would be to undermine the Bible's intent in expressing who He really is.

THE ONLY BEGOTTEN SON

All this helps us better understand the famous text John 3:16, which is used by those who deny the Trinity as a proof text against Jesus' eternal nature. It says, "God so loved the world that He gave His only begotten Son, that whoever believes in Him should not perish but have everlasting life."

The phrase "only begotten son" sure sounds as if Jesus once didn't exist and then came into

---

8   *God in Three Persons—in the New Testament;* Andrews University, May 2015

existence. But here's where we run into the limitations of human language—this time with the translation from one language to another. The Greek word *monogenes,* translated in the KJV, NKJV, and NASB as "only begotten," doesn't really mean "only begotten" as in being born—which implies once not existing. Rather, the term means "one of a kind" or "unique." It's about the nature of something, not about its creation. *Mono* in Greek means "one," such as in monotheism, and *genes* means "kind" or "type"; hence, one type or the like. The more astute translation does appear in other versions: "This is the way God loved the world: He gave his *one and only* Son" (NET); "God so loved the world that he gave *his one and only* Son" (NIV); "God so loved the world, that he gave *his only* Son" (ESV).

This confusion occurs because there is a similar Greek word, *gennao,* which means "beget" or "sire," and that verb has erroneously been applied to Jesus in John 3:16. In Hebrews 11:17, for example, we read, "By faith Abraham, when he was tested, offered up Isaac, and he who had received the promises offered up his only begotten son [*monogenes*]." *Only begotten son?* Didn't Abraham have other sons, Ishmael, and then later, with Ketura, more sons (Genesis 25:1–4)? So how could Isaac be called Abraham's "only begotten"?

He couldn't! The emphasis here was on the *unique status* of Isaac in that he was the son, the only son, who would be heir of the covenant promises made to Abraham.

In John 1:12–14, we can especially see the difference between the use of *genes* and *gennao*.

> As many as received Him, to them He gave the right to become children of God, to those who believe in His name: who were born, [*gennao*] not of blood, nor of the will of the flesh, nor of the will of man, but of God. And the Word became flesh and dwelt among us, and we beheld His glory, the glory as of the only begotten [*monogenes*] of the Father, full of grace and truth.

Look closely at what is happening here: Christians are "born/begotten," *gennao,* by God, which is how they get the right to become "children of God." But then, in verse 14, the apostle refers to Jesus as the *monogenes*, a different verb than *gennao*. John is not saying that, like Christians, Jesus is being born of God. That would be problematic, to say the least. Instead, he is emphasizing Jesus' unique status as the Son of God—something rather different than what happens to sinners who receive Jesus as their Messiah.

JESUS AS GOD

I believe the Scripture is clear about Jesus being the eternal God. Too many texts about Him make no sense otherwise. While many passages talk about His subordination to the Father, they do so in the context of His role as a human. And, yes, He manifested in the flesh, as the example of how we, too, should relate to God the Father. Ellen White was clear on this point:

> "His name shall be called Immanuel, ... God with us." "The light of the knowledge of the glory of God" is seen "in the face of Jesus Christ." From the days of eternity the Lord Jesus Christ was one with the Father; He was "the image of God," the image of His greatness and majesty, "the outshining of His glory." It was to manifest this glory that He came to our world. To this sin-darkened earth He came to reveal the light of God's love—to be "God with us." Therefore it was prophesied of Him, "His name shall be called Immanuel." [9]

Think through the implications were Jesus anything other than equal with the Father "from the days of eternity." We say the cross reveals God's love. How so? By God the Father, at some

---

9   *Desire of Ages*, pg. 19

point in the past, "bringing forth" Jesus for the purpose of being the sacrificial lamb for humanity's sins? If that were the case, the plan of salvation would be profoundly diminished because, in the end, it was not the eternal God dying on the cross for our sins but, instead, it was God creating a temporal being for the purpose of being thrown to the wolves. A nice gesture but, surely, something crucial is lost in the fact that it was Jesus' *destiny* to become human and die, as opposed to it being His *express selfless choice* to sacrifice His life for ours.

HOLY SPIRIT

◯ WHAT ABOUT THE HOLY SPIRIT?

All through Scripture, the deity of the Father is, of course, assumed. And, as we have seen, the scriptural evidence for the deity of Christ is likewise overwhelming. This, however, still leaves the question of the Holy Spirit. The word "Trinity" implies "three," so we need to deal now with the third person of the Godhead.

As with Jesus, the deity of the Holy Spirit has been questioned, challenged, and denied throughout church history. Arius (AD 265–336) rejected the full deity of the Holy Spirit and, through the centuries, various others have done the same. Today, the Mormons teach that the Holy Spirit is a divine being who is separate but not distinct from the Father. Jehovah's Witnesses claim that the Holy Spirit is a powerful but impersonal force, and certainly not an independent being. Various other views about the Holy Spirit are deemed by them to be unorthodox or outright heretical.

Nevertheless, Protestant Christianity affirms the deity of the Holy Spirit. To quote Wayne Grudem again: "God eternally exist as three persons, Father, Son, and Holy Spirit, and each person is fully God, and there is one God." [10]

I must concede that, in the Bible, the deity of the Holy Spirit is taught in more subtle terms than

---

10 *Systematic Theology,* Zondervan, 1994, p. 226

what is written clearly about the Son. Nothing comes right out in Scripture and says: *"The Holy Spirit is fully and completely God, just as the Father and the Son are."* Nevertheless, the evidence for the eternal divinity of the Holy Spirit is powerful, and many texts, as with the Son, become meaningless or confusing otherwise.

It's worth repeating that divine concepts are not easy for humans to grasp. The gap between the divine and us is truly infinite, and thus we're not going to easily forge that gap to fully understand Him, even after the Son became flesh and dwelt among us.

THE PERSONHOOD OF THE HOLY SPIRIT

In seeking to understand the deity of the Holy Spirit, we run into a question that we don't run into with Jesus: What is the personhood of the Spirit? Yes, we can understand the Father as a person; yes, we can understand the Son as a person, especially because Jesus Himself came to us as a human being. We can see the omnipresence of the Holy Spirit in Scripture, from the second verse in Genesis, where the Spirit hovers over the face of the waters, to the closing of Revelation, where the "Spirit and the bride say, 'Come'" (Revelation 22:17).

But the Spirit as a *person*?

Just as we can't take the words "Father" or the "Son" too literally, the same goes with the Holy Spirit. (Even the word "person," which we use for God, is itself limited in explaining exactly who God is.) We don't know God's exact nature as the Spirit. While Jesus says, "The wind blows where it wishes, and you hear the sound of it, but cannot tell where it comes from and where it goes. So is everyone who is born of the Spirit" (John 3:8), most likely human language can't fully grasp it anyway. Yet all through the Bible, especially in the New Testament, the personhood of the Holy Spirit is revealed.

The problem we encounter is that the Holy Spirit is occasionally depicted in impersonal terms—such as fire, water, or wind; therefore, some argue that He must be an impersonal divine force. He has been explained as something like an electric current that empowers us rather than as a being who interacts with us in a personal way. However, too many other texts refer to Him in ways that make sense only if He—as the Father and as the Son—is a divine person. Let's look at just a few of these verses.

> When He, the Spirit of truth, has come, He will guide you into all truth; for He will not speak on His own authority, but whatever He hears

He will speak; and He will tell you things to come (John 16:13).

The Helper, the Holy Spirit, whom the Father will send in My name, He will teach you all things, and bring to your remembrance all things that I said to you (John 14:26).

He who searches the hearts knows what the mind of the Spirit is, because He makes intercession for the saints according to the will of God (Romans 8:27).

I beg you, brethren, through the Lord Jesus Christ, and through the love of the Spirit, that you strive together with me in prayers to God for me (Romans 15:30).

God has revealed them to us through His Spirit. For the Spirit searches all things, yes, the deep things of God (1 Corinthians 2:10).

We see here that the Spirit speaks, guides, teaches, searches the heart, intercedes for us, and searches the deep things of God. The apostle Paul also talks about the "love of the Spirit." Can an impersonal force love? Doesn't love imply some kind of personhood? Indeed, it is persons, not electricity, who love. These texts make sense only if the Holy Spirit is a person and not merely a divine force.

There's more. As you read the following, ask yourself if these passages make it sound more like the Holy Spirit is being referred to as a person or as a mere force.

Do not grieve the Holy Spirit of God, by whom you were sealed for the day of redemption (Ephesians 4:30).

One and the same Spirit works all these things, distributing to each one individually as He wills (1 Corinthians 12:11).

Peter said, "Ananias, why has Satan filled your heart to lie to the Holy Spirit and keep back part of the price of the land for yourself?" (Acts 5:3).

Can you lie to and grieve an impersonal force? The idea of the Holy Spirit distributing gifts "as He wills" makes sense only if we are talking about a personal being. These terms of personality indicate that the Holy Spirit is self-knowing, self-willing, and self-determining. These texts could not be said to refer to some nebulous force or some impersonal, immaterial essence that only emanates from the Father or the Son.

Acts 15:28 reads, "It seemed good to the Holy Spirit, and to us, to lay upon you no greater burden than these necessary things." How does one make sense of this text were the Spirit only some impersonal influence? The writer could have easily substituted "God," "the Father," "Yahweh," or "Jesus" in place of "Holy Spirit" and it would have made sense. Instead, however, he used the phrase "Holy Spirit" to indicate another personal being, much as both the Father and Son are personal beings.

Ellen White is clear as well:

The Holy Spirit has a personality, else He could not bear witness to our spirits and with our spirits that we are the children of God. He must also be a divine person, else He could not search out the secrets which lie hidden in the mind of God. [11]

Sin could be resisted and overcome only through the mighty agency of the Third Person of the Godhead, who would come with no modified energy, but in the fullness of divine power. [12]

---

11   *Evangelism,* p. 617

12   *The Desire of Ages,* p. 671

The Holy Spirit, who is as much a person as God is a person, is walking through these grounds, unseen by human eyes; that the Lord God is our Keeper and Helper. He hears every word we utter and knows every thought of the mind. [13]

There are three living persons of the heavenly trio . . . the Father, the Son, and the Holy Spirit. [14]

One God composed of three persons—Father, Son, Holy Spirit. Indeed, the evidence for not just the personhood of the Holy Spirit, but His full divinity, is found in the Bible as well.

THE BAPTISM AND THE GREAT COMMISSION

For instance, in Luke 3:22, when Jesus was baptized, we learn, "The Holy Spirit descended in bodily form like a dove upon Him, and a voice came from heaven which said, 'You are My beloved Son; in You I am well pleased.'" Though this text in and of itself doesn't *prove* the divinity of the Holy Spirit, it does show all three persons—Father, Son, and Spirit—together, getting

---

13   *2SAT,* p. 136

14   *Evangelism,* p. 615

equal billing in the plan of salvation. And the next thing that happens, after Jesus' genealogy is outlined, is that Christ "was led by the Spirit into the wilderness" (Luke 4:1). Who but another member of the Godhead could lead a member of the Godhead anywhere?

And though we have looked at this text in the context of the divinity of Jesus, we also have the great commission pointing to the Holy Spirit: "Go therefore and make disciples of all the nations, baptizing them in the name of the Father and of the Son and of the Holy Spirit" (Matthew 28:19). Baptized in the name of the Father, who is God; the Son, who is God; and the Holy Spirit, who *is not God but just an impersonal force?* That doesn't make sense, does it? What does make sense is that the Holy Spirit is on par with the Father and the Son, regardless of the different function He plays in the plan of salvation.

LYING TO THE HOLY SPIRIT

The best way to understand the personhood and deity of the Holy Spirit is to see how He is portrayed in Scripture and then ask ourselves if these representations make sense if the Spirit were anything but God Himself.

In Acts chapter 5, for instance, we read that Ananias and Sapphira, who were members of the church, lied about a financial transaction. Let's let the text speak for itself:

> Peter said, "Ananias, why has Satan filled your heart to lie to the Holy Spirit and keep back part of the price of the land for yourself? While it remained, was it not your own? And after it was sold, was it not in your own control? Why have you conceived this thing in your heart? You have not lied to men but to God" (vv. 3, 4).

Look closely: The apostle Peter asks Ananias why he had lied to the Holy Spirit (v.3); he then says, "You have not lied to men but to *God*" (emphasis added). Peter equates the Holy Spirit with God. Ananias was not just lying to the apostles but to God Himself. Lying to the Holy Spirit is the same as lying to God. How does one make sense of what Peter said here if the Spirit was anything but fully God?

Also, what does one do with this statement by Jesus?:

> I say to you, every sin and blasphemy will be forgiven men, but the blasphemy against the Spirit will not be forgiven men. Anyone who speaks a word against the Son of Man, it will be forgiven him; but whoever speaks

against the Holy Spirit, it will not be forgiven him, either in this age or in the age to come (Matthew 12:31, 32).

My point here is not to examine what the unforgivable sin is; rather, I'm pointing at who is blasphemed and sinned against. Notice the parallel between "Son of Man" and "Holy Spirit." Both can be spoken against, but the difference is that speaking against the Holy Spirit is not forgivable.

Think about it: One can speak against Jesus, God the Son, and be forgiven. But one cannot speak against an impersonal force, the Holy Spirit, and be forgiven? How could speaking against something that is not God be blasphemous? Isn't blasphemy a sin against God? Indeed, the best way to understand these passages is to assume the divine personhood of the Spirit—just as we assume the deity and personhood of the Father and the Son.

DIVINE ATTRIBUTES

Even more powerful evidence exists for the divinity of the Holy Spirit. Once again, these texts make sense only if the Holy Spirit is God.

The author of Hebrews 9:14 asks, "How much more shall the blood of Christ, who through the eternal Spirit offered Himself without spot to

God, cleanse your conscience from dead works to serve the living God?" The Spirit is eternal—and 1 Timothy 6:16 says that only God has "immortality," another way of saying that only God is eternal. But here Hebrews gives that unique attribute to the Holy Spirit. How could that be if the Holy Spirit is not God?

One form of logic is called a syllogism. It works like this: All men are mortal. Socrates is a man. Therefore, Socrates is mortal. Makes sense, right? In parallel, if God alone is eternal, and the Holy Spirit is eternal, then we can know that the Holy Spirit is God!

And what about Isaiah 40:13, 14?

Who has directed the Spirit of the Lord, or as His counselor has taught Him? With whom did He take counsel, and who instructed Him, and taught Him in the path of justice? Who taught Him knowledge, and showed Him the way of understanding?

The questions in this passage are rhetorical, because Isaiah knows the answer to each one. And the answer to each one is that no one can do these things for the Spirit of the Lord because He is God. If one substituted "the Spirit of the Lord" with "God" or "Yahweh," it would read almost the same: "Who has directed Yahweh?" In contrast, if "the Spirit of the Lord" were replaced with "an impersonal force," it would be problematic:

> Who has directed the *impersonal force?* Or as *its* counselor has taught *it?* With whom did *it* take counsel, and who instructed *it,* and taught *it* in the path of justice? Who taught *it* knowledge, and showed *it* the way of understanding?

Again, this text doesn't make sense were the Holy Spirit anything other than fully God. Let's look at a few more.

While addressing Israel, Isaiah wrote, "They rebelled and grieved His Holy Spirit" (63:10). Look, though, at these following texts about the same thing: "The LORD said to Moses: 'How long will these people reject Me? And how long will they not believe Me, with all the signs which I have performed among them?' " (Numbers 14:11). And: "The LORD alone led him, and there was no foreign god with him" (Deuteronomy 32:12).

The Lord alone was the God who led them in the wilderness, and yet when Isaiah talks about their rebellion against Him, He is referred to as "the Holy Spirit." This works fine—but only if the Holy Spirit is God!

In 1 Corinthians 3:16, Paul says, "You are the temple of God." Then in 1 Corinthians 6:19, just a few verses later, Paul says, "Your body is the temple of the Holy Spirit." Temple of God is equated to the temple of the Holy Spirit. That makes sense *unless* Paul is saying that we are "the temple of God" and we are "the temple of an impersonal force emanating from God."

Earlier, while looking at the divinity of Jesus, I quoted a text and showed that we could substitute any person of the Godhead for another and the passage worked fine. Here is the passage again but in the context of the divinity of the Holy Spirit:

I beg you, brethren, through the Lord Jesus Christ, and through the love of the Spirit, that you strive together with me in prayers to God for me (Romans 15:30).

Remember, God, Jesus, and Spirit are linked. So let's look at that same text but switch the various places where the three persons are placed.

I beg you, brethren, through the Spirit, and through the love of God, that you strive together with me in prayers to the Lord Jesus Christ for me.

That reads just fine, doesn't it? That's because all three persons are fully divine. The testimony of Scripture is certain: The Holy Spirit is God, just as the Father and the Son are God.

DIFFERENT ROLES, DIFFERENT PERSONS, ONE GOD

We have seen that there is one God manifested as three persons. They are one, yet they are distinct, each one playing a unique role in the plan of our salvation.

I once heard a pastor put it this way, "God the Father *initiates* the plans, God the Son *executes* the plans, and God the Holy Spirit *applies* the plans." Thus, our salvation is so crucial that all three persons of the Godhead are involved in it—with, of course, Jesus the Son, God Himself, dying on the cross for our sins.

The divinity of Jesus is central to the gospel. Because He is fully divine, we can know God as a person and enter into a deeper, saving relationship with Him. How much clearer could the Bible make it in John 14:6–9? Jesus said,

> "I am the way, the truth, and the life. No one comes to the Father except through Me. If you had known Me, you would have known My Father also; and from now on you know Him and have seen Him." Philip said to Him, "Lord, show us the Father, and it is sufficient for us." Jesus said to him, "Have I been with you so long, and yet you have not known Me, Philip? He who has seen Me has seen the Father; so how can you say, 'Show us the Father'"?

If Jesus were nothing more than a created messenger from God, and not God Himself, we could know only what he *taught* about God; this is much different than *knowing* God in person, as we can know Him through Jesus—but only because He is God. The Lord wants us to know Him as a person and so He came to us as a person so we could understand.

Not only that, He is the person who died in our stead. How much more complete could our redemption be? In Christ "all the fullness" of God was pleased to dwell (Colossians 1:19); this means that it was God Himself who, in Christ, reconciled us to Himself (2 Corinthians 5:18, 19) by being our sin-bearer at Calvary.

It's worth stressing again: If Jesus had been less than God, a mere created being like us, then God sent a lesser being in His place, a lesser being to die for us on the cross. Contrast that thought with the idea of God Himself, in Christ, dying for us on the cross. We see what is lost if the divinity of Jesus is lost. We lose everything, actually.

And the Holy Spirit's role is equally crucial because, after Jesus ascended to heaven, we can know Jesus as a person only because of the work of the Holy Spirit in revealing Jesus to us—not an impersonal force revealing Jesus, but another person of the Godhead doing it for us.

This is what Jesus was telling us in John 14–16 and what the Bible teaches about how the prophets were inspired by the Holy Spirit. (See 1 Peter 1:11 and 2 Peter 1:21.) We know the truths we know only because the Holy Spirit, God Himself, reveals these truths to us. Who could better reveal God to us than, indeed, God Himself? Respected theologian Paul Petersen writes,

It is also the Holy Spirit who by sanctifying the saints in Christ (1 Corinthians 1:2; 1 Peter 1:2) applies the merits of the sacrifice and atonement of Jesus. As Jesus is our intercessor in the heavenly sanctuary (Hebrews 7:25), the Holy Spirit comes to us on earth as the intercessor (Romans 8:26) to help us pray with the attitude and mind of Jesus, connecting us while still on earth to God in heaven. He is able do that because He is one with God and knows the depth of the very being of God (1 Corinthians 2:10). Sanctifying us in Christ, the Spirit reaps in our lives a harvest of love, peace, joy, etc. (Galatians 5:22, 23), thus reconciling us with God by applying the merits of the sacrifice of Calvary. [15]

---

15 *God in Three Persons—in the New Testament;* Andrews University, May 2015

There is One God composed of three distinct Persons, all intricately involved in the plan of our salvation. It doesn't get any better than that!

THE PLAN OF OUR SALVATION

We look out at the cosmos and marvel. The idea of billions of stars in just the Milky Way boggles our brains. And astronomers tell us that there are more galaxies in the cosmos than we have brain cells between our ears. Keep in mind—this just represents the galaxies that astronomers are able to observe, which may represent only a fraction of the entire universe!

How do we comprehend this miracle?

Yet even more miraculous, something even more difficult to wrap our minds around, is that the God who created all those galaxies loves us so much that He immersed Himself thoroughly in the plan of our salvation. Yet if we can't fully comprehend His creation, how could we fully expect to comprehend the Creator Himself in terms of His nature and the depths of His love and our salvation? The fact is, we can't.

But we can know that the Father, the Son, and the Holy Spirit—one God, one singular name—had one purpose in regard to us: our salvation. And our salvation was so crucial, so central, that all three persons of the Godhead were involved.

God gave us the best; He gave us Himself in order to implement and fulfill the plan of redemption, the plan of *our* salvation. And it took all of them—the Father, the Son, the Holy Spirit—working together to do it.

Thus, we can in complete confidence end with the words Paul used to end his second letter to the Corinthians: "The grace of the Lord Jesus Christ, and the love of God, and the communion of the Holy Spirit be with you all. Amen" (13:14).

APPENDICES

THE TRINITY IN 24 NEW TESTAMENT VERSES

1. MATTHEW 3:16

"When He had been baptized, Jesus came up immediately from the water; and behold, the heavens were opened to Him, and he saw the Spirit of God descending like a dove and alighting upon Him."

2. MATTHEW 12:28

"If I [Jesus] cast out demons by the Spirit of God, surely the kingdom of God has come upon you."

3. MATTHEW 28:19

"Go therefore and make disciples of all the nations, baptizing them in the name of the Father and of the Son and of the Holy Spirit."

4. LUKE 1:35

"The angel answered and said to her, 'The Holy Spirit will come upon you, and the power of the Highest will overshadow you; therefore, also, that Holy One who is to be born will be called the Son of God.' "

5. LUKE 3:22

"The Holy Spirit descended in bodily form like a dove upon Him [Jesus], and a voice came from heaven which said, 'You are My [the Father's] beloved Son; in You I am well pleased.' "

6. JOHN 14:26

"The Helper, the Holy Spirit, whom the Father will send in My [Jesus'] name, He will teach you all things, and bring to your remembrance all that I said to you."

7. JOHN 15:26

"When the Helper comes, whom I [Jesus] shall send to you from the Father, the Spirit of truth who proceeds from the Father, He will testify of Me."

8. ACTS 1:4

"Being assembled together with them, He [Jesus] commanded them not to depart from Jerusalem, but to wait for the Promise of the Father, 'which,' He said, 'you have heard of from Me.'"

9. ACTS 2:33

"Therefore being exalted to the right hand of God, and having received from the Father the promise of the Holy Spirit, He [Jesus] poured out this which you now see and hear."

10. ACTS 10:38

"God anointed Jesus of Nazareth with the Holy Spirit and with power, who went about doing good and healing all who were oppressed by the devil, for God was with Him."

11. ROMANS 1:4

"Declared to be the Son of God with power according to the Spirit of holiness, by the resurrection from the dead."

12. ROMANS 8:9

"You are not in the flesh but in the Spirit, if indeed the Spirit of God dwells in you. Now if anyone does not have the Spirit of Christ, he is not His."

13. ROMANS 14:17, 18

"The kingdom of God is not eating and drinking, but righteousness and peace and joy in the Holy Spirit. For he who serves Christ in these things is acceptable to God and approved by men."

14. 1 CORINTHIANS 6:11

"Such were some of you. But you were washed, but you were sanctified, but you were justified in the name of the Lord Jesus and by the Spirit of our God."

15. 1 CORINTHIANS 12:4–6

"There are diversities of gifts, but the same Spirit. There are differences of ministries, but the same Lord. And there are diversities of activities, but it is the same God who works all in all."

16. 2 CORINTHIANS 13:14

"The grace of the Lord Jesus Christ, and the love of God, and the communion of the Holy Spirit, be with you all."

17. GALATIANS 4:6

"Because you are sons, God has sent forth the Spirit of His Son into your hearts, crying out, 'Abba! Father!'"

18. EPHESIANS 1:17

"That the God of our Lord Jesus Christ, the Father of glory, may give to you the spirit of wisdom and revelation in the knowledge of Him."

19. EPHESIANS 2:18

"For through Him we both have access by one Spirit to the Father."

20. EPHESIANS 2:22

"In whom [Jesus] you also are being built together for a dwelling place of God in the Spirit."

21. TITUS 3:6

"Whom [the Holy Spirit] He poured out on us abundantly through Jesus Christ our Savior."

22. HEBREWS 9:14

"How much more shall the blood of Christ, who through the eternal Spirit offered Himself without spot to God, cleanse your conscience from dead works to serve the living God?"

23. 1 PETER 1:2

"According to the foreknowledge of God the Father, in sanctification of the Spirit, for obedience and sprinkling of the blood of Jesus Christ: Grace to you and peace be multiplied."

24. REVELATION 1:4, 5

"John, to the seven churches which are in Asia: Grace to you and peace from Him who is and who was and who is to come, and from the seven Spirits who are before His throne, and from Jesus Christ, the faithful witness, the firstborn from the dead, and the ruler over the kings of the earth."

APPENDICES

THE TRINITY IN THE WRITINGS OF ELLEN WHITE

In 1850, Ellen G. White confirmed the person-hood of Jesus Christ and God the Father, stating, "I have often seen the lovely Jesus, that He is a *person*. I asked Him if His Father was a person and had a form like Himself. Said Jesus, 'I am in the express *image* of My Father's *person*'" (*Early Writings,* 77, emphasis is in original).

"We have been brought together as a school, and we need to realize that the Holy Spirit, who is as much a person as God is a person, is walking through these grounds, that the Lord God is our keeper, and helper. He hears every word we utter and knows every thought of the mind" (*Manuscript 66,* 1899, p. 4).

"Sin could be resisted and overcome only through the mighty agency of the Third Person of the Godhead, who would come with no modified energy, but in the fullness of divine power" (*The Desire of Ages*, 671.2).

"What gift could Christ bestow rich enough to signalize and grace His ascension to the mediatorial throne? It must be worthy of His greatness and His royalty. Christ gave His representative, the third person of the Godhead, the Holy Spirit. This Gift could not be excelled" (*Christ Triumphant*, 301.4).

"The Holy Spirit has a personality, else He could not bear witness to our spirits and with our spirits that we are the children of God. He must also be a divine person, else He could not search out the secrets which lie hidden in the mind of God. 'For what man knoweth the things of a man, save the spirit of man which is in him? Even so the things of God knoweth no man, but the Spirit of God' " (*Evangelism*, 617.1).

"In Christ is life, original, unborrowed, underived. 'He that hath the Son hath life.' 1 John 5:12. The divinity of Christ is the believer's assurance of eternal life" (*The Desire of Ages*, 530.3).

In 1897/1898, Ellen White made her first statement regarding the personhood of the Holy Spirit, stating that He was "the third person of the Godhead" (*Special Testimonies*, Series A10 25, 37). Similarly, she wrote that the Holy Spirit was "the Third Person of the Godhead" in 1898 in *The Desire of Ages* (p. 530, 671).

AMAZING FACTS

AMAZING DISCIPLES
— ONLINE —

AN E-COURSE BY THE
AMAZING FACTS CENTER OF EVANGELISM

LEARN ANYTIME. ANYPLACE. ANYWHERE.
Affordable, Convenient & Empowering Online Bible Training

Your training will focus on Jesus' method of evangelism, giving Bible studies, answering objections, conducting church prophecy seminars, finding and leading seekers from interests to baptism—but that's just the tip of the iceberg of what you'll learn, gain, and experience!

Course includes live Q&A sessions with
Pastor Doug Batchelor and Amazing Facts evangelists!

Get the details by signing up for our "notify me" list at

AmazingDisciples.com

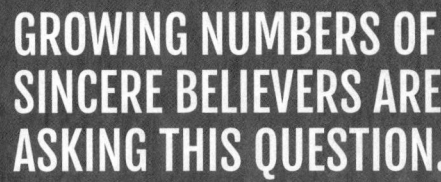